Better Homes and Gardens®

ON THE FARM

Hi! My name is Max. I have some great projects to show you—and they're all about farms! We're going to have lots of fun making them together.

Inside You'll Find...

A barnyard matching game.

Animal Friends

Hey, look! Max is feeding the ducks. His friend Elliot is milking the cow. What animal is drinking some milk? Which one of the sheep is different from the others? Which duck is different?

4

Did you know...

● Most farm animals eat and drink a lot more than you do. In just one day, a dairy cow drinks about a bathtubful of water and eats as much food as an entire family of four people would eat in three days!

● Farm animals eat grass, hay, silage (chopped plants stored in a silo), corn, and grain.

● Most farmers buy food for their animals at the feed mill, a store that's like a supermarket for farmers. It sells food for all sorts of animals, from chickens to cows.

● Animals like the taste of salt, so farmers put out blocks of salt for the animals to lick.

● Do you have a sheep in your closet? Maybe you do. Farmers give sheep haircuts, known as shearing. The cutoff hair is wool, which is made into sweaters and coats.

● Has a dog ever told you he's hungry by pushing his bowl around the floor, or a cat "said" she's angry by swishing her tail? Animals communicate in ways other than words, although we can't always understand them.

Shake this up when you're in the m-o-o-d for a treat.

Moo-Cow Milk Shake

Max likes to drink milk, and he loves to eat ice cream, so he puts both in his favorite drink. Milk is good for Max, and for you, too. For a vanilla shake, leave out the chocolate syrup.

What you'll need...

- Vanilla ice cream
- Ice-cream scoop
- One 2-cup-size plastic jar with tight-fitting lid
- Spoon
- Chocolate syrup
- Milk
- Tall glass

1 With adult help, remove vanilla ice cream from freezer. Allow it to sit on the counter at room temperature about 15 minutes or until it is soft enough to scoop. Scoop ice cream into the jar till half full.

2 Add some chocolate syrup to ice cream in the jar. Pour milk into the jar until it is about ¾ full. Mix with a spoon.
   (If you prefer a vanilla shake, leave out the chocolate syrup.)

3 Put the lid onto the jar and tighten. (A screw-top jar works best because you can shake without spilling.) With adult help, shake hard till ice cream and milk are mixed (about 3 minutes). Remove the jar lid. Pour the milk shake into a glass. Makes 1.

SHAKE

SHAKE

SHAKE

Pick a Flavor

You can makc any flavor of milk shake you want.
- Add some peanut butter to the shake for a Choco-Nutty Milk Shake.
- Add some strawberry preserves or thawed, undrained frozen strawberries to the vanilla shake for a Strawberry Milk Shake.

Pastel-colored cotton balls give this old favorite a new look.

Calico Sheep

Your make-believe farmyard can be filled with colorful sheep. Use soft cotton balls in different colors to make calico, or spotted, sheep.

What you'll need...

- Pencil
- One 8½ × 11-inch piece of sturdy paper
- Scissors
- White crafts glue
- Sheep Decorations (see tip on page 9)
- Crayons
- Cotton balls
- 2 spring-type clothespins

1 For the sheep's head, draw a small oval on the paper. Draw a big oval for the sheep's body (see photo). With scissors, carefully cut out your sheep. Glue the head to the body, overlapping the edges slightly. Draw the sheep's eyes and nose with crayon. If you want, glue on ears and a tail (see Sheep Decorations, page 9).

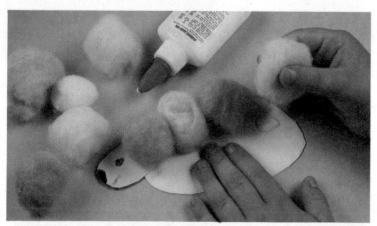

2 Put some glue on one side of the sheep's body. Spread it around. Place one cotton ball at a time on the glue (see photo). Place the cotton balls close together so the entire side is covered. Then turn the sheep over and repeat on the other side. Let dry.

3 Make the sheep's legs by clipping two clothespins to the bottom of your animal (see photo). If you wish, decorate clothespin legs with crayons.

Sheep Decorations

● Cut small ears and a tail from construction paper or felt, and then glue onto your sheep.

● Besides crayons, try markers or tempera paint to decorate wood clothespins. Plastic clothespins make great legs for your sheep because they are already brightly colored.

Kids have fun putting these little porkers together.

Piggy Biscuits

You can eat these funny-looking pigs. Shape the peanutty biscuit dough into pigs, bake them, and then serve them warm.

What you'll need...

- Rolling pin
- Piggy Biscuit Dough (see page 31)
- Flour
- One 2½-inch round cutter
- Milk
- Custard cup
- Pastry brush
- Small spoon
- Bottle opener
- Raisins, tiny chocolate pieces, or nuts
- Shortening
- Baking sheet

1 Roll or pat the Piggy Biscuit Dough to ½-inch thickness on a lightly floured surface. For the pigs' bodies, cut dough into 5 circles with round cutter (see photo).

2 To make pig faces, roll small pieces of the extra dough into small balls for the ears, noses (snouts), and feet. Pour a small amount of milk into custard cup. Brush each piece with milk to help it stick to the pig's body and face.

Roll a small piece of dough on the counter (see photo) to make a "snake" for a pig's tail.

3 To finish the pig faces, make cheeks by cutting deeply into the dough with a spoon. Use the pointed end of a bottle opener to cut the snout and mouth.

Carefully place the Piggy Biscuits on a greased baking sheet. Use raisins to make eyes (see photo). With adult help, bake in a 450° oven about 6 minutes. Makes 5 biscuits.

Did you know...

● People often think that pigs don't care what they eat. But actually, they are better able to taste food than people are. Pigs have more taste buds than we do, and they can detect small differences in flavors.

● Pigs are used for hunting in France because they have very sensitive noses. They are trained to hunt truffles, a special mushroom, by sniffing in the woods for them.

Help Max find his way through the maize.

Things That Go

Max's corn is so high he can't find his way back to the barn. Which way does Max need to drive his tractor to go feed the animals? Use your finger to trace the path Max should follow.

Household castoffs become home-crafted farm toys.

Farm Tractor and Wagon

A farmer uses a tractor and a wagon to haul food for his animals and straw for their beds. If you were a farmer, what would you carry in your wagon?

What you'll need...

- 2 gelatin or small cereal boxes
- Scissors
- White crafts glue
- Tempera paint or construction paper
- 2-inch piece of a plastic drinking straw
- 8 jar lids or large buttons
- Tape
- 1 piece of yarn or string, about 6 inches long

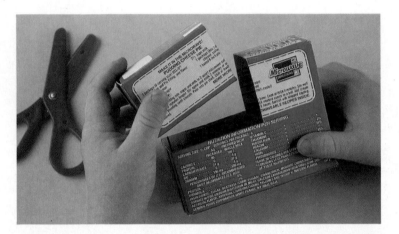

1 With adult help, cut out the upper corner of one of the boxes for the tractor (see page 31). Slide the corner you've cut out down into the larger part of the box, forming a hood for the tractor. Glue in place.

For the wagon, cut off the front or back side of the other box. The remaining sides form the bed of the wagon.

2 Decorate the boxes by painting them or covering them with construction paper. Make a window for the tractor out of paper. Glue it in place. Make an exhaust pipe for the hood of the tractor by cutting a hole in the cardboard and sticking in a piece of plastic straw. Glue jar lids in place for wheels. Let dry about 1 hour.

3 Turn the tractor on its side and the wagon upside down. Tape one end of the piece of yarn to the bottom of the tractor and the other end to the wagon.

Tractor Tips

Look around your house for items that you can use to make your tractor special.
● For wheels, collect milk-jug caps or lids from glass jars. Or, use the bottom of a paper or plastic-foam cup.
● Use a bendable straw or piece of pasta for the exhaust pipe.

Paper Pickups

Pickup trucks are handy for going places and moving things. A farmer may drive his pickup to town to go to the bank or pick up feed for his animals. Fill yours with things you like.

What you'll need...

- 1 sheet and 1 smaller piece of construction paper or poster board
- Pencil
- Scissors
- Milk-jug cap or one of similar size
- White crafts glue
- Old magazines or pictures of you or your family

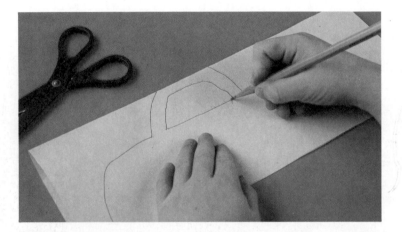

1 Fold the whole sheet of paper in half lengthwise. Crease the fold well. Place fold at top. Draw the shape of a pickup truck on the paper (see photo). The top of the cab should be on the fold. Cut out the pickup truck. Do not cut across the top of the cab. If you want, have an adult cut out the cab window.

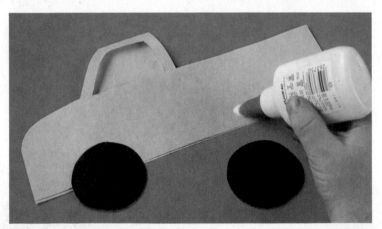

2 To make the wheels, place the milk-jug cap on the small piece of construction paper. Trace around the cap to make a circle. Make 4 circles for wheels. Cut out the circles. Glue 2 on one side of the pickup. Turn the truck over. Glue the remaining 2 on the other side.

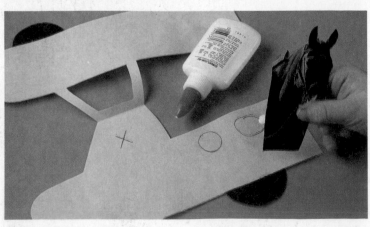

3 Look through old magazines and cut out pictures of a driver and things you like. Flip open the folded paper. Have an adult draw an "X" in the cab where the driver should be glued and circles in the bed of the pickup where the other pictures should be glued (see photo). Glue pictures onto your pickup. Flip folded paper closed.

Play a barnyard hide-and-seek game.

In the Barnyard

Something is hiding in Max's feed sack. Can you tell what it is?
Other items are hidden in funny places in the barnyard. Can
you find the mouse? Ear of corn? Rake? Cat? Bucket?

Spark imaginations with recycled cardboard containers.

Barn and Silo

A barn makes a good home for some farm animals. Their food is stored in a silo. You can build a play barn and silo out of boxes.

What you'll need...

- 2 empty shoe boxes
- 1 round oatmeal box
- Construction paper
- Tape or white crafts glue
- Crayons or markers
- Scissors
- Construction paper or paper plate

1 For the barn, find a box that is a square or rectangle. If you can't find a large enough box, stack two smaller boxes of the same size. Glue them together. Let dry.

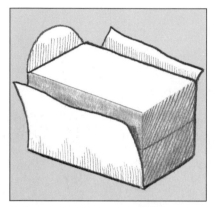

2 Cover the outside of the box with paper. For roof support, cut domed ends (see drawing). Tape.

3 Make a roof by taping a piece of construction paper to the box (see drawing). Decorate the barn any way you want.

4 To make silo, decorate a sheet of paper any way you wish. Cover outside of oatmeal box with the construction paper. Tape the paper.

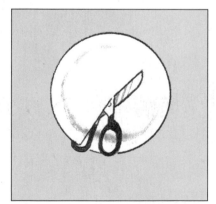

5 To make roof, draw circle on paper. Using your scissors, cut it out. Make 1 cut from anywhere on outside edge of circle straight to center.

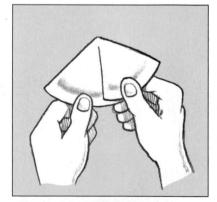

6 Hold 2 edges where you cut slit. Overlap to form a cone. Tape to hold. Tape roof to silo. For shingles, glue small pieces of paper on roof.

Farm Buildings

Have you ever wondered what all the buildings on a farm were for?

- A chicken coop is where the hens lay their eggs.
- A milk house is where the milk is stored.
- The machine shed is where tractors, wagons, and other farm equipment and tools are kept.

Wooden crafts sticks keep the farm animals corralled.

Stick Fence

Max builds fences to keep his horses inside his field, his cows out of the corn, and the pigs out of the garden. What animals would you keep inside your fence?

What you'll need...

- ● Tape
- ● Waxed paper
- ● Jumbo crafts sticks
- ● Glue
- ● Masking tape

1 Tape a piece of waxed paper to the counter. Lay 2 crafts sticks about 4 inches apart. Put a small dot of glue about ½ inch from one end of each stick. Using another crafts stick, lay one end on one dot of glue and the other end on the other dot of glue. Repeat with more glue and another crafts stick to form a square (see photo).

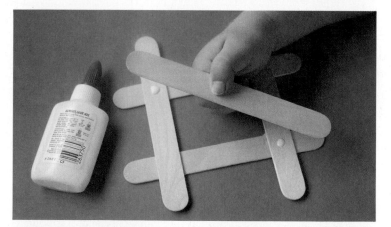

2 Press the sticks gently until the glue starts to stick. Glue a crafts stick on the bottom of one post and the top of the next post (see photo) to connect. Press for a few seconds. Let dry.

3 If you would like to make several sections of fence, you could fence in a pasture or have a corral. Join the sections together with a small piece of tape on the back side of the fence. This will help it stand.

Fence-Building

If you want to make a gate, use a piece of pipe cleaner instead of tape to connect two fence sections, so the gate swings open.

Twist one end of the pipe cleaner around the top of a fence post. Make a loop on the other end of the pipe cleaner, and slip it over the top of another post.

Things That Grow

Max hoes his garden to get rid of the weeds so his vegetables have more room to grow big. Count how many different kinds of vegetables are growing in his garden. Which is your favorite?

24

Dried soup beans make a pretty flower mosaic.

Soup-er Flowers

Soup beans come in all shapes, sizes, and colors. Arrange them to make beautiful flowers. Or, create a terrific picture of whatever you like.

What you'll need...

- 1 package of assorted soup beans
- Custard cups
- Crayons or tempera paint
- Poster board, cardboard, or construction paper
- White crafts glue

1 Empty the soup beans from the package into custard cups. Draw a picture of a flower with a stem and leaves on the poster board (see photo). Squeeze some glue onto the flower. Rub the glue around to evenly cover the inside of the flower.

2 Pick out the beans you like (for seeds, see tip on page 27). It's fun to use ones that have different colors, shapes, and sizes. Place the beans on the glue-covered flower any way you like (see photo). Let dry.

Max knows where to find soup beans. Look for bags of different kinds of soup beans on the supermarket shelf where they have dried beans.

Seed Flowers

Assorted seeds, such as melon, squash, sunflower, or large pearl tapioca, may be used instead of soup beans. You can make an even greater variety of pictures using seeds because they come in so many different shapes, colors, and sizes.

It's fun to make cards of your own for a special day.

Veggie-'n'-Fruit Cards

What's more fun than giving someone you like a card? Making the card yourself, that's what! And you can decorate the card by "printing" it with vegetables and fruits.

What you'll need...

- Vegetables and fruits
- Kitchen knife
- Cutting board
- Paper plate
- Waxed paper
- Tempera paint
- Paintbrushes
- Construction or watercolor paper, folded in half
- A jar filled with water
- Paper towels

1 To make printing stamps, ask an adult to cut the vegetables or fruits into halves, or other desired shapes and sizes (see page 32).

2 Cover your work area with waxed paper. Dip the cut side of the vegetable or fruit into the paint on a paper plate. (Or use a brush to paint the cut edge. Keep your brush in water between paintings.) Be careful not to get too much paint on your vegetable or fruit. Make a print on an extra sheet of paper to get rid of some of the paint.

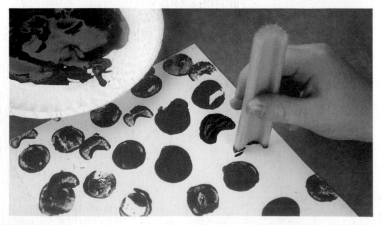

3 Lay the vegetable or fruit onto the paper and press lightly to get a copy or "impression." Lift off the vegetable or fruit. You can get two or three prints before you need more paint. (Be careful not to jiggle the fruit or vegetable on the paper, or the design will smear.) Let your card dry. Write a message inside the card.

Parents' Pages

We've filled this special section with more activities, recipes, reading suggestions, hints we learned from our kid-testers, and many other helpful tips.

Animal Friends

See pages 4 and 5

Activities like the one on page 4 help teach the concept of similarities and differences. Your children see the fun activity as a game, and it helps develop the perceptual skills needed to learn how to read.

Moo-Cow Milk Shake

See pages 6 and 7

Making our Moo-Cow Milk Shake helps show children what cows provide. You also can try making butter.

Start with heavy whipping cream and have your children pour it into a plastic jar with a tight-fitting lid. Secure the lid and let the children take turns shaking the jar. When small curds of butter form (after

about 5 minutes of shaking), drain off the liquid, and rinse the butter under cold running water, squeezing gently.

Add a little salt, if you wish. Sample your butter on bread.

Calico Sheep

See pages 8 and 9

The sheep are fun to make because of the fuzzy cotton balls. You can help your children make a whole farmyard of animals (see page 23). An oval could also be a pig. A rectangle with rounded corners could be the body of a horse or cow.
- Reading suggestion:
Nattie Parsons' Good-Luck Lamb
by Lisa Campbell Ernst

Piggy Biscuits

See pages 10 and 11

Our kid-testers loved making these home-baked porkers. They took artistic license in creating their own creatures. The pigs pictured on page 11 are made from Piggy Biscuit Dough, a whole wheat biscuit studded with peanuts.

As a nifty shortcut, substitute refrigerated biscuit dough. Directions for both methods follow.

Piggy Biscuit Dough

- ¾ cup all-purpose flour
- ¼ cup whole wheat flour
- 1 tablespoon brown sugar
- 1½ teaspoons baking powder
- ⅛ teaspoon salt
- ¼ cup shortening
- ¼ cup finely chopped peanuts
- ¼ cup milk

- In a medium mixing bowl stir together all-purpose flour, whole wheat flour, brown sugar, baking powder, and salt.
- With a pastry blender cut in

the shortening till the mixture resembles coarse crumbs. Stir in chopped peanuts.
- Make a well in the center of the flour mixture. Add milk all at once. Stir with a fork till the dough clings together.
- Turn dough out onto a lightly floured surface. Knead gently for 10 to 12 strokes.
- Follow the directions on page 10 for making the Piggy Biscuits.

Quick Piggy Biscuits
- Open a 7½-ounce can of refrigerated biscuits, and separate biscuits. Place 5 biscuits evenly spaced on a lightly greased baking sheet. Use the remaining biscuits for ears, snouts, tails, and feet.
- Follow directions given on page 10 for assembling the Piggy Biscuits. Bake in a 450° oven for 6 to 8 minutes.

Things That Go

See pages 12 and 13

Max's corn is so high that he needs help finding his way out of the maize. His maize is field corn, the type of corn animals eat. The type you buy to eat is sweet corn or popcorn.

Farm Tractor And Wagon

See pages 14 and 15

Here's a tip for you that we learned when we developed this project. To make box cutting easier and neater, open the box flaps. Cut from the edge of the flaps toward the center of the box. Re-glue flaps before fitting corner inside the larger part of the box in Step 1.

Paper Pickups

See pages 16 and 17

Our staff noted that during kid-testing some children needed more help in the placement of pictures in their pickups. You may want to draw a horizontal line for your children about 1 inch below the top edge of the pickup bed as a guide. Have them place the pictures above the line so they show when the truck is folded.

In the Barnyard

See pages 18 and 19

Visiting a farm is a great way for children to gain an appreciation of animals firsthand. Many zoos and theme parks have petting farms so children can touch the animals. Contact your state's department of tourism or Farm Bureau office for information.

Barn and Silo

See pages 20 and 21

You probably have some cardboard boxes and tubes around your home that will make a wonderful barn and silo for your children to play with. A shoe box is an old standby, but don't forget lightweight cardboard boxes like bakery and frozen food boxes that are easier to cut.

If the boxes need to be taller, stack them and wrap with masking tape.

Stick Fence

See pages 22 and 23

It's easy to make cotton-ball animals to keep inside stick fences. Use cotton balls as the base, and then add feet, bills, eyes, noses, and tails made from construction paper or felt. A little glue holds everything together.

Things That Grow

See pages 24 and 25

Children love to watch things grow. But sometimes youngsters get frustrated waiting to see results. To keep interest from waning, try a quick-growing item, such as a carrot top in a shallow dish with a little water (sprouts in about three days), herbs in small pots placed on a windowsill (usually about a week), or alfalfa sprouts in a jar (two or three days).

● To grow alfalfa sprouts, buy alfalfa seeds that have not been chemically treated at a garden store or in the produce department of your grocery store. Add 2 tablespoons of the seeds to a quart jar. Fill the jar halfway with warm water and let soak overnight. Throw away the floating seeds, because they won't sprout.

● Cover the mouth of the jar with a piece of cheesecloth or woven fabric secured with a rubber band, and pour off the water. Rinse the seeds with warm water and drain.

● Lay the jar on its side and put in a warm closet. Rinse three times a day.

● After the seeds have sprouted leaves, place the jar in the light for a day. When the leaves turn green, they are ready to eat in a sandwich or salad.

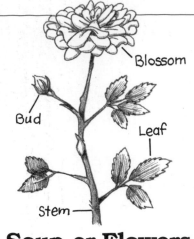

Blossom

Bud

Leaf

Stem

Soup-er Flowers

See pages 26 and 27

For young children, you may prefer to purchase packages of a single type of bean, such as limas, which are large and easy to handle.

Depending on the season and where you live, seeds may be a thrifty option. Buy seeds in bulk at the garden store, or use expired seeds from a previous year. Be sure any seeds used for a crafts project have not been chemically treated.
● Reading suggestions:
Your First Garden Book
by Marc Brown
Spring Things
by Mary Kunir

Veggie-'n'-Fruit Cards

See pages 28 and 29

Your children will get a whole new perspective of vegetables and fruits when they start considering what size and shape of print each one will make.

Making Prints

Here are some ideas for using fruits and vegetables for other printing projects:
● Make wrapping paper for gifts using an ear of corn or broccoli.
● Preserve and display your child's artwork on a potholder. Use paint from a crafts store designed for fabric to print a 9-inch square of 100-percent cotton muslin. When the design is dry, heat-set it by ironing. Place a layer of quilt batting between the stenciled square

and a plain one. Outline the shapes with stitching. Trim with bias tape.

Round

Oval

Big   Small   Long

Try radishes, cauliflower, mushrooms, peppers, zucchini, potatoes, and squash.

The paint will stick to the cut surfaces better if you allow the cut vegetables and fruits to dry on paper towels for about an hour before using. (Let lem-

ons and oranges air-dry overnight on the counter.)

Kids enjoy expressing themselves, so encourage them to "write" messages on their cards even if they can't write. Ask your children to read their messages back to you.

BETTER HOMES AND GARDENS® BOOKS
Editor: Gerald M. Knox
Art Director: Ernest Shelton
Managing Editor: David A. Kirchner
Department Head, Food and Family Life: Sharyl Heiken

ON THE FARM
Editors: Sandra Granseth and Heather M. Hephner
Graphic Designers: Harjis Priekulis and Linda Ford Vermie
Editorial Project Manager: Angela K. Renkoski
Contributing Illustrator: Buck Jones
Contributing Photographer: Scott Little

Have BETTER HOMES AND GARDENS®
magazine delivered to your door.
For information, write to:
ROBERT AUSTIN
P.O. BOX 4536
DES MOINES, IA 50336